# The Story of
# MOZI

www.royalcollins.com

*Picture Story Book of
Ancient Chinese Thinkers*

# The Story of MOZI

Shao Jiasheng

Translated by Wu Meilian

Picture Story Books of Ancient Chinese Thinkers
The Story of MOZI

Shao Jiasheng
Translated by Wu Meilian

First published in 2024 by Royal Collins Publishing Group Inc.
Groupe Publication Royal Collins Inc.
550-555 boul. René-Lévesque O Montréal (Québec) H2Z1B1 Canada

Copyright © Jinan Publishing House Co., Ltd.
This English edition is authorized by Jinan Publishing House Co., Ltd.

All rights reserved. Without limiting the rights under copyright reserved above, no part of this publication may be reproduced, stored in or introduced into a retrieval system, or transmitted in any form or by any means (electronic, mechanical, photocopying, recording, or otherwise), without the prior written permission of both the copyright owner and the above publisher of this book.

ISBN: 979-8-9852490-5-7

To find out more about our publications, please visit www.royalcollins.com.

From a young man who fell from a wealthy family to becoming a pioneering thinker, Mozi's, life was marked by generosity and legend.

His ideal was universal love, and his pursuit was anti-aggression.

His wisdom, eloquence, and skills shine brightly and vividly in the interweaving of ink and colors.

Let's experience his thoughts of rationality and universal love together and ponder the "chivalry" and "righteousness" in his heart.

The ancestor of Mozi was Muyi, courtesy name Ziyu. He was a prince and a high official of the State of Song during the Spring and Autumn Period. After Muyi's death, his son Gongsun You and grandson Yushi in turn succeeded his post.

In 576 BCE, a coup took place among the nobilities of Song. Yushi failed and retreated to a place called Pengcheng.

In 572 BCE, the States of Song, Jin, and other vassal states besieged Pengcheng. Yushi surrendered to the State of Jin and was assigned to a place called Huqiu in Jin. The family thus settled in Jin, and their migration was remembered in history.

One descendant later moved to the State of Xiaozhu (today's Zaozhuang, Shandong Province) and gradually lost their noble titles.

Around 468 BCE, Mozi was born into this commoner family. He was a shepherd boy and a carpenter's apprentice when he was a child. Despite the difficult living conditions, he received a certain degree of education.

However, as time went by, Mozi felt the need to expand his knowledge, so he was determined to visit and study with famous teachers and learn how to rule a country.

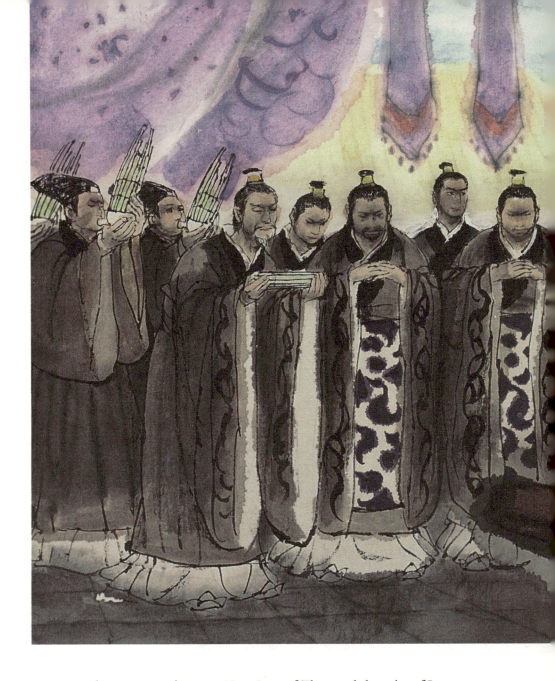

Upon the agreement between King Ping of Zhou and the ruler of Lu, Shi Jiao, an official in charge of state rituals, was sent to teach sacrificial ceremonies in the State of Lu, and his descendants remained in the country. Therefore, the ritual and music system of the Zhou Dynasty was passed down in the State of Lu.

Mozi learned about the rites of Zhou with the descendants of Shi Jiao and studied the *Book of Songs*, the *Book of Documents*, and etiquette like other Confucian scholars.

Through studying, Mozi developed doubts about Confucianism and its overly complicated etiquette. He eventually abandoned this school of thought and continued to travel around in search of his ideal ideological doctrine. During this process, Mozi collected many classics and brought them back home to study.

Mozi not only studied political literature but also combat techniques from military books, and he practiced martial arts according to the needs of the times. After a period of intensive research, he gradually formed his own opinions. He decided to leave home and promote his ideas. With a sword on his back and the ambition of saving the world in his heart, Mozi set off on an arduous journey.

Mozi promoted his ideas and received disciples, such as Qingu Li, Gao Shizi, and Gao He. The Mohists began to grow into a powerful group. Mozi required his disciples to not only study literature but also combat skills like himself. This was intended to better protect their personal safety as well as to stop violence.

Mozi was very strict with his disciples. Once, he got angry at his disciple Geng Zhuzi, who felt wronged and asked, "Don't I have anything better than others that deserves your approval?"

Mozi answered, "If you go to the Taihang Mountains with a horse and an ox to draw your carriage, which animal will you use your whip on?"

Geng Zhuzi replied, "The horse, of course."

"Why so?" asked his master.

He said, "Because a good horse is worth the motivation and challenge."

Mozi said, "I also think you are worth the motivation and challenge."

Mozi never stopped studying, even during his journey. On their way to the State of Wei, Mozi's disciples were surprised by the great number of books on the cart and asked about the purpose of bringing books.

Mozi said, "The Duke of Zhou used to read one hundred articles every morning and meet with seventy scholars in the evening. That was why he could assist the king in ruling the country, and his name is still remembered today. I do not have state responsibilities nor farming duties; how dare I not study with all the time I have?"

Mozi quickly gained the trust of the Duke of Lu and became his important counselor, providing advice on both state affairs and family issues. One day, the duke asked Mozi how to avoid the State of Qi's attack.

Mozi first told the stories of benevolent and tyrant kings in the Xia, Shang, and Zhou dynasties. Then, he said, "Respect Heaven and worship the ghosts and gods, be good to your people, and form an alliance with your neighboring states with generous gifts. You can thus avoid the disaster by having the whole country work together for the same goal."

The Duke of Lu had two sons; one was a devoted learner, and the other was very generous. The duke did not know who should be appointed as the crowned prince, so he asked Mozi for advice. Mozi said, "We cannot tell at this point yet. Maybe they are just behaving in such for the sake of reward and reputation."

"For example, a fisherman does not bend his back just to thank the fish he catches; a man does not use food as bait just because he loves rats. I hope Your Majesty can examine the princes' motivations and what they do together."

Mozi was traveling from the State of Lu to the State of Qi and visited a friend on his way. The friend said, "No one in the world talks about benevolence and righteousness anymore except you. You should stop your pursuit."

Mozi said, "If only one out of ten people is farming while the other nine are idling, then the farmer should only work harder to provide for everyone. It is exactly because few people value benevolence and righteousness that those who do should work harder. Otherwise, the world will only be even more chaotic."

After bidding farewell to his friends, Mozi set off for the State of Qi in the north. On his way, he met a fortune teller who told him, "On this day in history, the Emperor of Heaven killed the black dragon in the north. Your skin has turned black, so you cannot go to the north." Mozi ignored him and continued his journey. But when he reached the Zishui River, he could not cross and had to return.

The fortune teller said, "I told you not to go to the north."

Mozi replied, "Right now, no one south of Zishui can go north, and no one north of Zishui can go south. Some of them have dark skin, and some of them have fair skin, but why can none of them get where they want? The Emperor of Heaven has killed the green, red, white, and black dragons in the east, west, south, and north. If what you said was true, then no one in the world is allowed to go anywhere." The fortune teller could not answer that.

Mozi and his disciples were in the State of Chu. At that time, the Chu people and the Yue people were fighting on a river. Lu Ban* made a weapon called the *gouxiang*, with a hook to pull the enemy's ships back when they retreated and a shield to resist the enemy's ships when they advanced. With the *gouxiang*, the Chu people defeated the Yue people, and Lu Ban was very proud of his creation. Mozi, however, was dismissive about Lu Ban's bragging and retorted the fact that his creation had caused aggression and death.

---

\* Lu Ban was an excellent craftsman who lived during the late Spring and Autumn Period and the beginning of the Warring States Period. His tribe's surname was Ji, and he belonged to the Gongshu family under this tribe. He was thus also known as Gongshu Ban, Gongshu Pan, Ban Shu, or Lu Ban.

Lu Ban did not listen to Mozi. After Mozi left, he had an audience with the King of Chu and quickly won the latter's trust with his outstanding craftsmanship.

He then made another combat tool called the *yunti*, the "ladder for the king."

Around 440 BCE, the State of Chu planned to attack the State of Song. Mozi was very worried about this, so he asked his eldest disciple, Qingu Li, to lead 300 men to help defend the State of Song, and he personally went to dissuade the King of Chu from sending troops.

Mozi traveled day and night; his shoes were torn, and his feet were frayed. Ten days later, he arrived at Ying, the capital of Chu State (today's Jiangling area in Hubei Province). He immediately met with Lu Ban.

Mozi said to him, "A man from the north offended me, and I want you to help me kill him. I will give you ten taels* of gold as a reward."

Lu Ban answered, "I have morals and do not kill without reason." Hearing this, Mozi seized the opportunity and questioned him about helping the King of Chu to attack the State of Song.

---

\* Tael is an ancient Chinese weight unit, and one tael equals 50 g.

"The State of Song is not at fault. You are not dissuading the King of Chu but helping him with the aggression, causing innocent people to be killed. This is not morality," he said.

Lu Ban agreed and took Mozi to King Hui of Chu.

Mozi questioned, "If a man gives up his gorgeous carriage to steal other people's old cart, gives up his rich clothes to steal other people's shabby clothes, and gives up his exquisite meals to steal other people's leftovers, what do you think of him?"

King Hui immediately replied, "He must have an addiction to stealing."

Mozi said, "The State of Chu is rich in land and products, while the State of Song is small and scarce in resources. The differences between the two countries are like that between a luxurious carriage and a broken cart or between brocade and rags. Won't it make Your Majesty the same as the man addicted to stealing if you attack the Song? It is immoral, and you are bound to fail."

King Hui looked back at Lu Ban, then he turned to Mozi and said, "You are right, but Lu Ban has already built the siege equipment for me. I must attack Song."

So Mozi requested to compete with Lu Ban, who accepted the challenge. Mozi used his belt to imitate a city wall, and Lu Ban used wood chips to build a miniature *yunti* ladder.

A simulated war began, and both sides used their hands to imitate soldiers' movements. Lu Ban was very confident at first, but he was soon defeated by Mozi's defensive weapons.

Lu Ban was unwilling to admit his failure. He kept changing his tactics and attacked nine more times, but all of them were defeated by Mozi. Finally, Lu Ban ran out of siege equipment, but Mozi still had many ways to defend. Unwillingly, Lu Ban said to Mozi, "I know how to defeat you, but I won't tell." King Hui was confused and asked him what he meant.

Mozi said, "What he meant was to kill me, but my disciple Qingu Li and his three hundred men are waiting for you on the wall of Song." King Hui was afraid and gave up his plan to attack.

Before Mozi left Chu, Lu Ban said to him, "Before I met you, I wanted to attack Song. But now, I will never do such an unjust act anymore."

After this, Mozi presented a letter to King Hui of the State of Chu to state his views, which the king approved but still politely rejected. He was only willing to provide Mozi with daily necessities but was not willing to adopt his theories. Mozi refused King Hui's support and said, "I hear that virtuous people do not accept reward if their advice is not implemented, and they do not stay in the court if their advice is not accepted. Please let me leave then."

King Hui did not see Mozi off, using his old age as an excuse, but instead sent Minister Mu He. Mozi explained his ideas to Mu He, who greatly appreciated them. However, he said to Mozi, "What you said does make sense. But the king is the master of the state. He may not adopt it because of your low status."

Mozi replied, "As long as the advice is useful, why care who offered it? If an herb can cure the illness of a king, why not let him take it just because it is a grass?"

Knowing that he would not be able to implement his ideals in Chu, Mozi left the state and continued his journey.

Luyang Wenjun,* a minister of Chu, said to King Hui, "Mozi is a sage from the north. If you don't meet with him or don't give him gifts, you will lose an important talent."

---

\* Luyang Wenjun, or Gongsun Kuan, was the grandson of King Ping of Chu. He served as a high military official in the third year of King Ping of Chu (526 BCE) and was granted a fiefdom in Luyang, today's Lushan, Henan Province.

So, King Hui sent him to chase Mozi back with an offer of fiefdom, but Mozi did not accept it.

Sometime later, Mozi heard that the State of Chu was planning to attack the State of Zheng, so he came to Chu again and met with Luyang Wenjun.

Mozi asked him what he would do if the cities in his fiefdom got into a fight and the big cities invaded the small ones. "I will punish them without mercy," answered Luyang Wenjun.

Mozi thus pointed out that his attack against the State of Zheng was wrong. Luyang Wenjun did not understand, "Why so? The people of Zheng have killed three of their rulers consecutively, and the Gods have condemned them. I am only punishing them on behalf of the Gods."

Mozi then asked, "If a father hits his son, and the neighbor's father joins him in the punishment, saying he is offering help, is that acceptable?" Luyang Wenjun thought for a long time and agreed.

Through constant travels, Mozi's team grew bigger and bigger. Mozi and his fellow Mohist disciples traveled around the states to promote their ideas.

Mozi sent disciple Gongshang Guo to lobby the King of Yue. The king highly appreciated his opinions and asked him to invite his master Mozi to Yue with rewards of fiefdom.

Gongshang Guo took the Yue envoy and rich gifts to Mozi. He happily told Mozi about his experience in the State of Yue and the king's wish to invite Mozi to his state.

Mozi, however, was not as excited as his disciple, "We cannot judge the size of the reward. We should see whether the King of Yue really values our suggestions." Gongshang Guo fell silent and secretly sent the envoy back to Yue.

Mozi sent disciple Gao Shizi to lobby the King of Wei. The king respected him and awarded him with a high position and salary. Gao Shizi served the king wholeheartedly, but his advice was never adopted. Eventually, Gao Shizi left the State of Wei.

Gao Shizi found Mozi in the State of Qi and asked, "I gave the King of Wei many suggestions, but he never accepted them, so I left. Do you think the king will blame me for being too arrogant?" Mozi was very happy to hear this and explained to him the importance of upholding morality. He called Qingu Li and other disciples over and said, "Listen. I have often heard that people abandon morality and pursue good fortune, but today, Gao Shizi allowed me to see how a person can give up wealth and pursue morality."

Mozi became a high official in the State of Song when Duke Zhao of Song was on the throne. But this ruler, who highly respected Mozi, was assassinated by Huang Xi, who established himself as the ruler of the Song. Although Huang Xi had great power, he was worried about being criticized and was always wary of Mozi. In the end, he found an excuse to imprison Mozi.

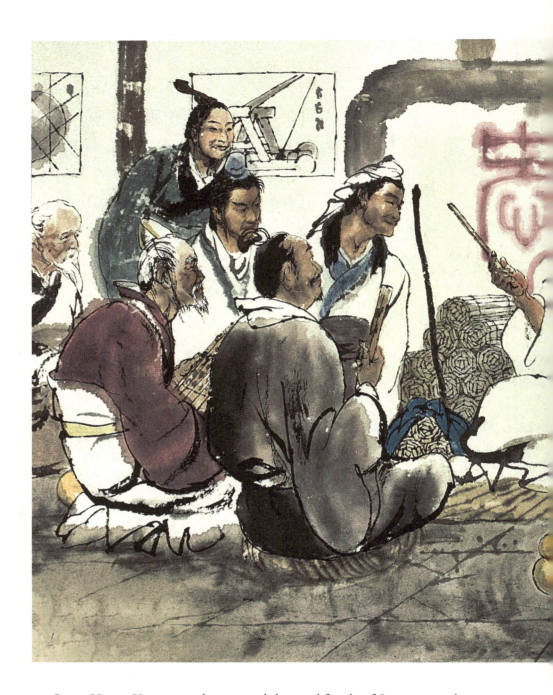

Later, Huang Xi was overthrown, and the royal family of Song regained power and released Mozi.

Despite his difficult time in Song, Mozi never lost confidence in the goal he pursued and continued to preach and teach.

In his later years, Mozi had many disciples, such as Qingu Li, Gao He, Xian Zishuo (also known as Xian Zishi), and Gongshang Guo. These outstanding Mohists were highly respected by all states wherever they visited and preached.

In the last days of his life, Mozi urged his disciples to persevere for morality despite temporary setbacks in the chaotic world. He looked around at his disciples and left the world with regret.

Born in a lower-class family, Mozi lived a hard life and knew a lot of practical skills, such as physics, mathematics, and mechanical manufacturing.*

---

\* Mozi achieved outstanding results in geometry, optics, mechanics, kinematics (a branch of mathematics), etc. The records on optical issues in the *Mojing* systematically explain the relationship between light and shadow, pinhole imaging, and various specular reflection imaging issues.

Mohism and Confucianism were known as the two eminent schools of thought at that time. The Mohists were against extravagant etiquette and advocated frugality, which was in line with the poor people's needs.

After Mozi's death, the Mohist school he founded split into three sects: the Xiangli school, the Xiangfu school, and the Dengling school, who all believed that they had obtained the true inheritance of Mozi. With the changes of the times, the Mohists lost their past glory and gradually disappeared. However, Mozi's constant pursuit of truth and his thoughts will never be forgotten.

## ABOUT THE AUTHOR

Shao Jiasheng is a Chinese painting and comic artist. His representative works in Chinese painting include *Autumn Scenery at Yandang Mountain, Water Town in Jiangnan, Tai Gong Fishing, Various States of Ji Gong*, etc. He has created a hundred comic strips. His paintings are realistic and meticulous, with a unique and captivating style, and he has won many awards.